Piano • Vocal • Guitar

BEST OF
HARRY NILSSON

Cover Photo by Michael Putland/Getty Images

ISBN 978-1-4950-1671-4

HAL•LEONARD®
CORPORATION
7777 W. BLUEMOUND RD. P.O. BOX 13819 MILWAUKEE, WI 53213

Visit Hal Leonard Online at
www.halleonard.com

AS TIME GOES BY

Words and Music by
HERMAN HUPFELD

when two lov-ers woo, they still say, "I love you," on that you can re-ly;

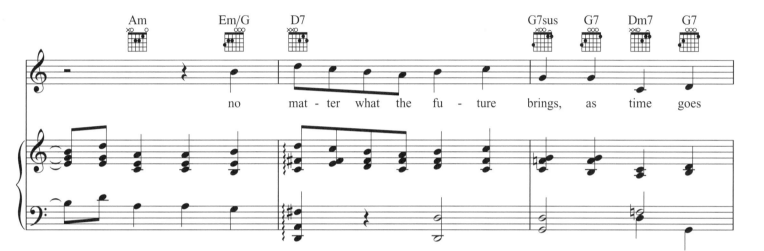

no mat-ter what the fu-ture brings, as time goes

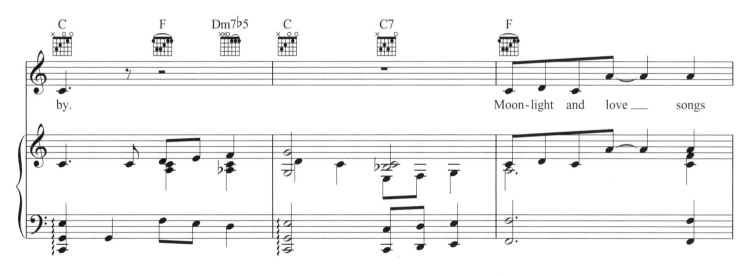

by. Moon-light and love___ songs

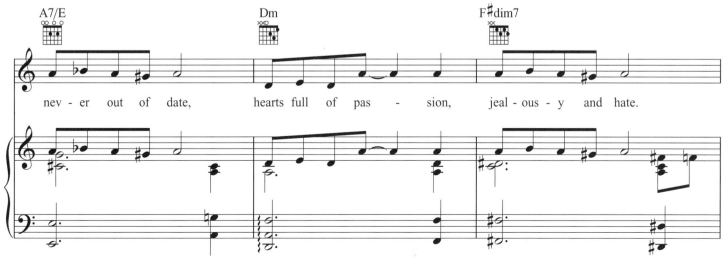

nev-er out of date, hearts full of pas-sion, jeal-ous-y and hate.

Wom-an needs man ___ and man must have his mate, that no one can de-

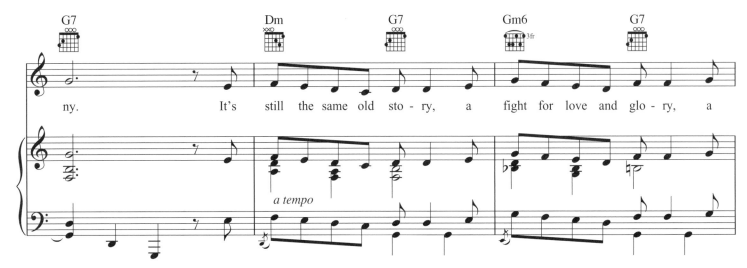

ny. It's still the same old sto-ry, a fight for love and glo-ry, a

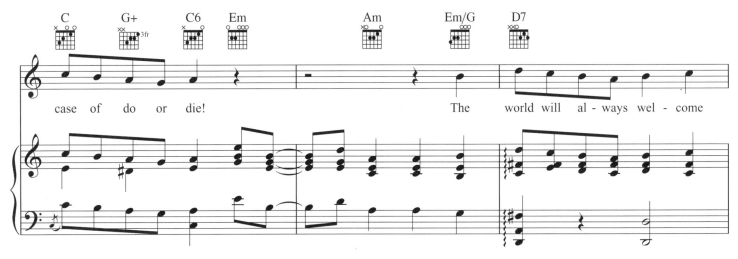

case of do or die! The world will al-ways wel-come

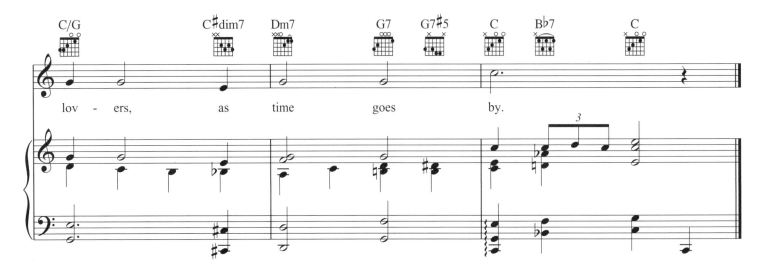

lov-ers, as time goes by.

EVERYBODY'S TALKIN'
(Echoes)
from MIDNIGHT COWBOY

Words and Music by
FRED NEIL

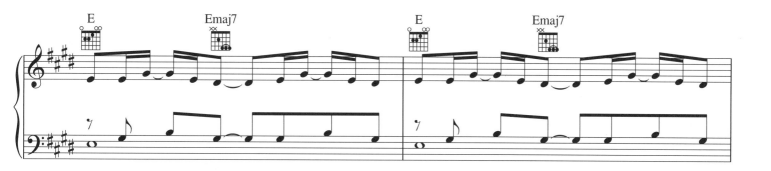

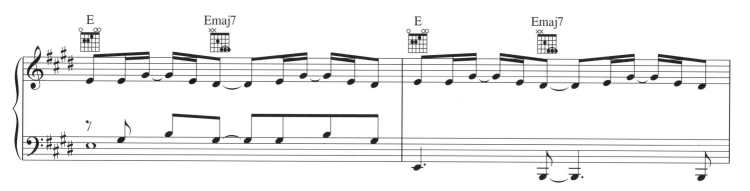

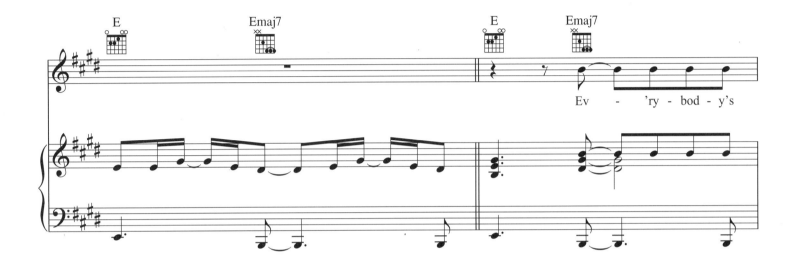

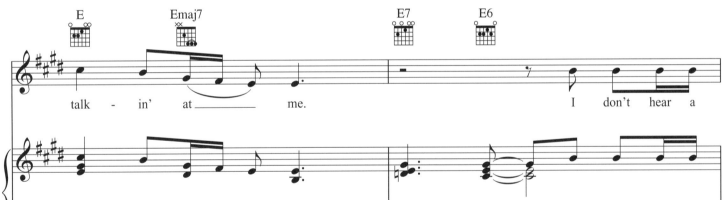

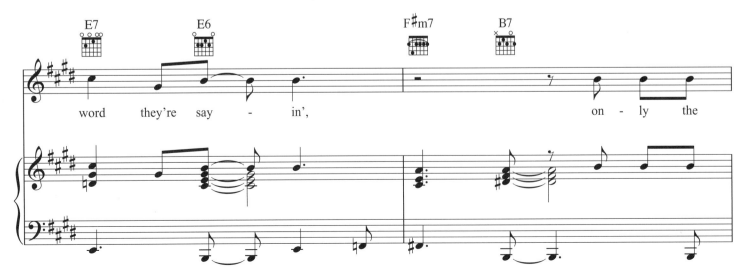

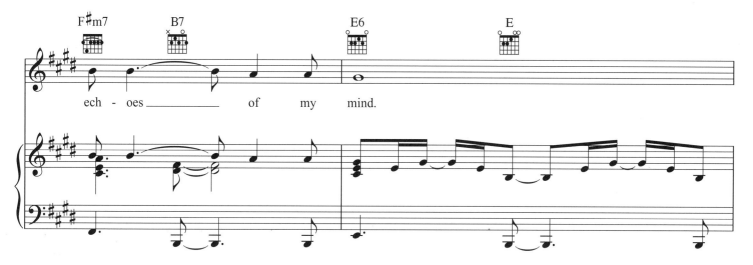

ech - oes _____ of my mind.

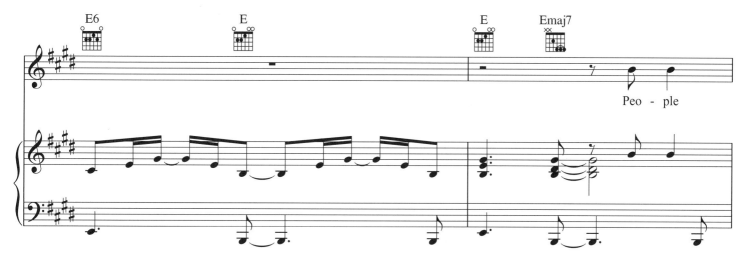

Peo - ple

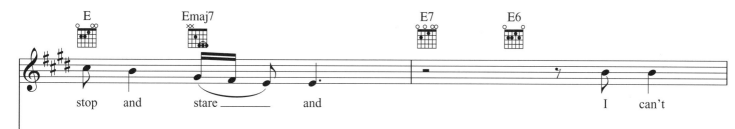

stop and stare _____ and   I can't

see their fac - es,   on - ly the

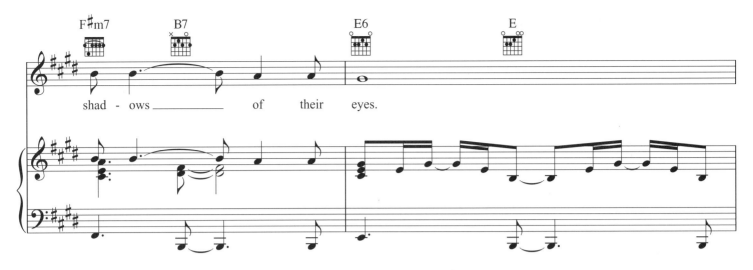

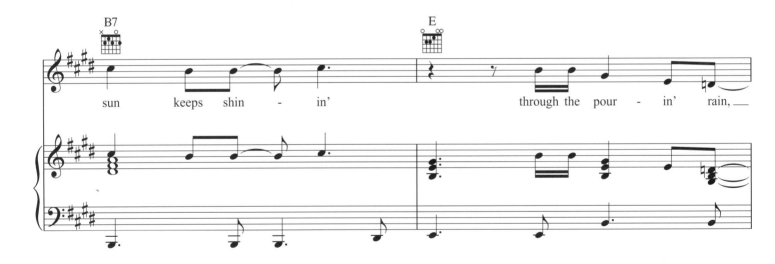

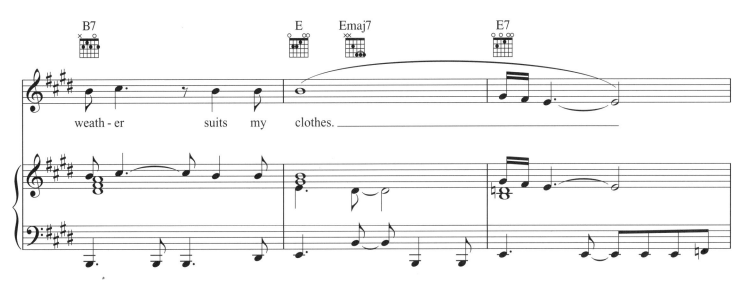

weath-er suits my clothes. _____

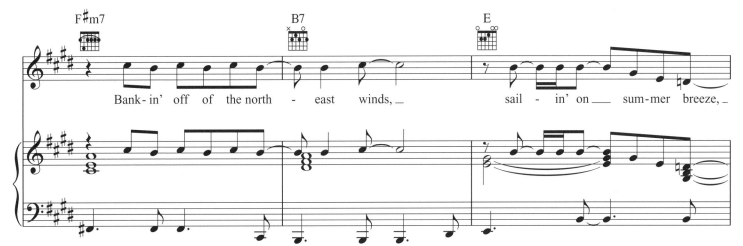

Bank-in' off of the north - east winds, __ sail - in' on __ sum-mer breeze, __

and skip-pin' o - ver the o -

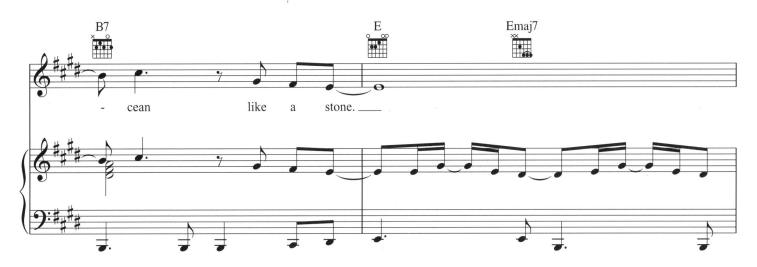

- cean like a stone. __

CODA

Ev - 'ry - bod - y's talk - in' at _____ me. _____

Repeat and Fade

Ah. _____

Optional Ending

COCONUT

Words and Music by
HARRY NILSSON

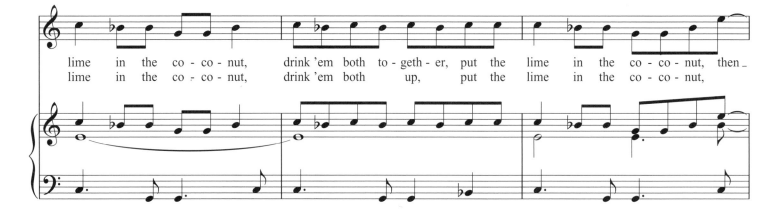

lime in the co-co-nut, drink 'em both to-geth-er, put the lime in the co-co-nut, then
lime in the co-co-nut, drink 'em both up, put the lime in the co-co-nut,

To Coda

____ you feel bet-ter. Put the lime in the co-co-nut, drink 'em both up. Put the
drink 'em both up. Put the lime in the co-co-nut, drink 'em both up. Put the

lime in the co-co-nut, call me in the morn-ing. Ooh, ____ ooh, ____

D.S. al Coda

____ ooh; ____ ooh, ____ ooh, ____ ooh. ____ ____ ooh. ____

CODA

lime in the co-co-nut. You're such a sil-ly crab. Put the lime in the co-co-nut,

drink 'em both to-geth-er, put the lime in the co-co-nut, then___ you feel___ bet-ter. Put the

lime in the co-co-nut, drink 'em both up. Put the lime in the co-co-nut,

Repeat and Fade

call me in the morn - ing.
Yes, if you call me in the morn-ing, I'll tell___ you what to do. Yes, if you

GOTTA GET UP

Words and Music by
HARRY NILSSON

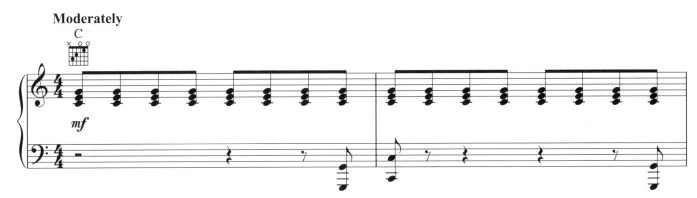

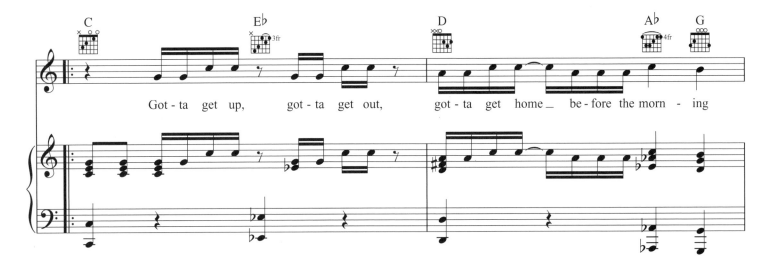

Got-ta get up, got-ta get out, got-ta get home _ be-fore the morn - ing comes.

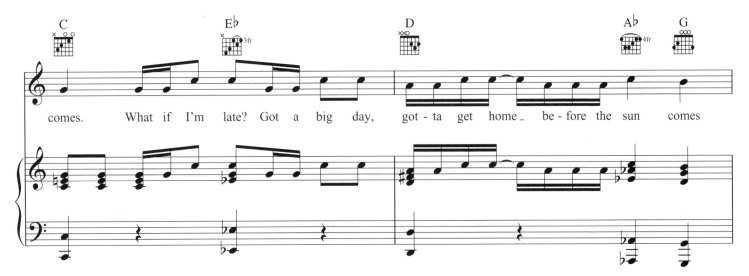

comes. What if I'm late? Got a big day, got-ta get home _ be-fore the sun comes

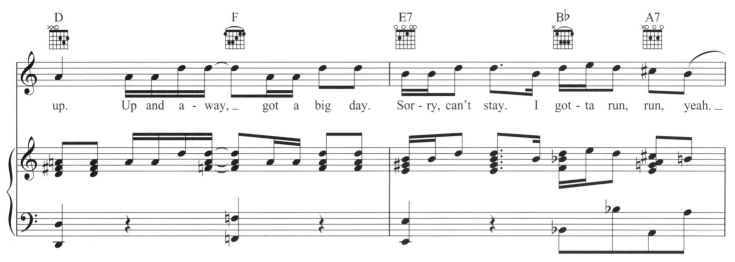

up. Up and a-way,__ got a big day. Sor-ry, can't stay. I got-ta run, run, yeah.__

__ Got-ta get home,__ pick up the phone, got-ta let the peo-ple know I'm gon-na be late.__

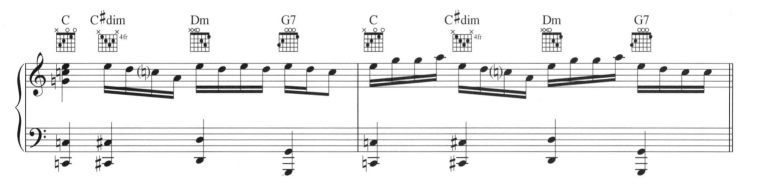

1. There was a time,__ when we could dance un-til a quar-ter to ten.__ We nev-er thought it would
2. (See additional lyrics)

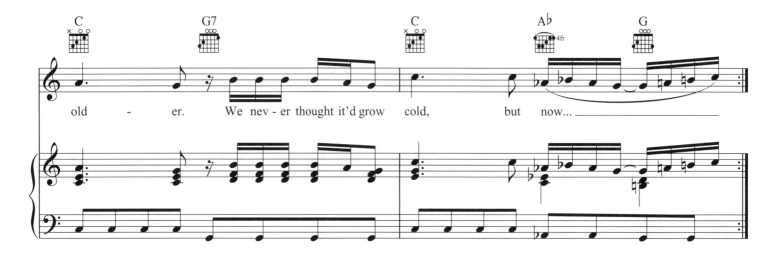

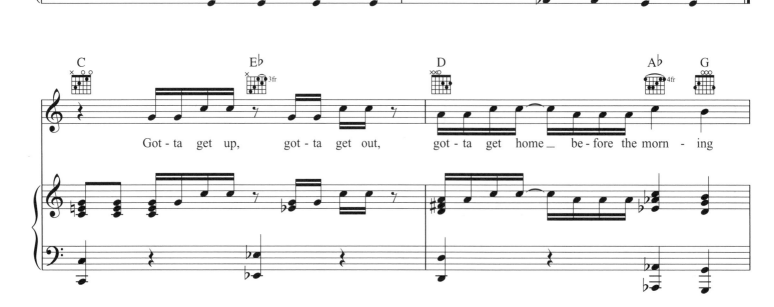

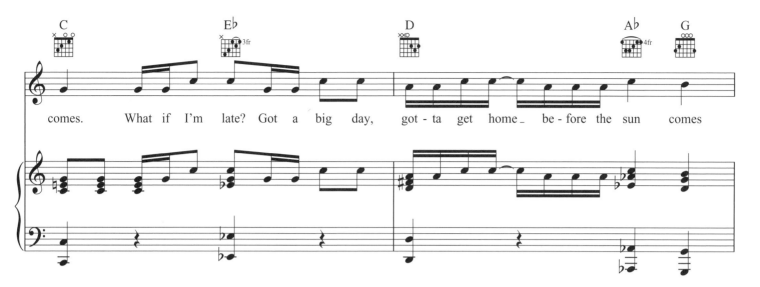

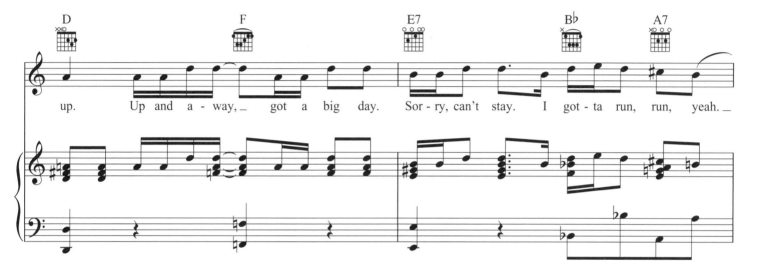

Additional Lyrics

2. Down by the sea, she knew a sailor who had been to war.
She never even knew a sailor before.
She never even knew his name.
He'd come to town and he would pound her for a couple of days,
And then he'd sail across the bubbly waves.
And those were happier days, but now...

JUMP INTO THE FIRE

Words and Music by
HARRY NILSSON

Moderately fast

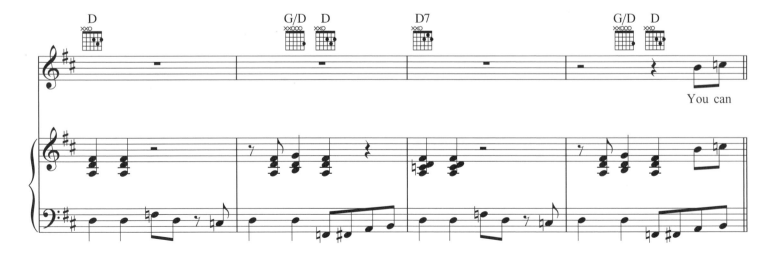

You can

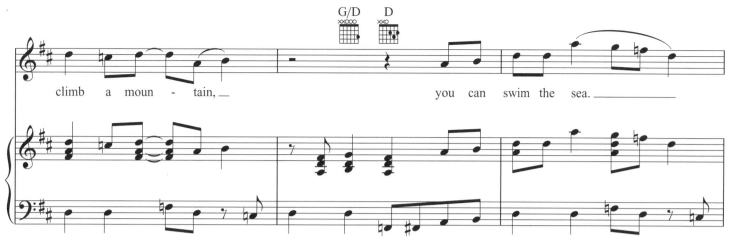

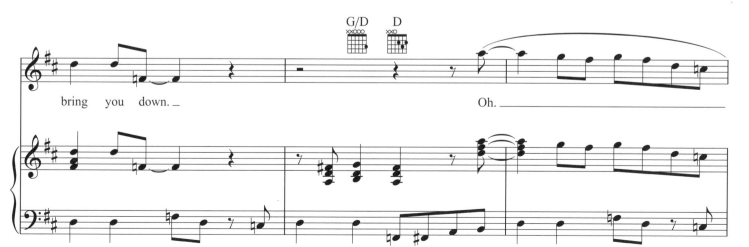

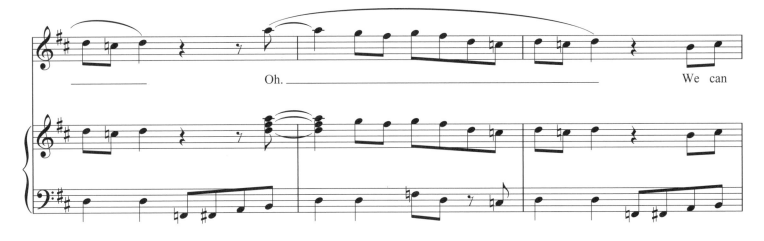

Oh. _____ We can

make each oth - er hap - py. Oh, we can make each oth - er hap - py. ____

_____ We can make each oth - er hap - py. We can

make each oth - er hap - py.

(I Guess)
THE LORD MUST BE IN
NEW YORK CITY

Words and Music by
HARRY NILSSON

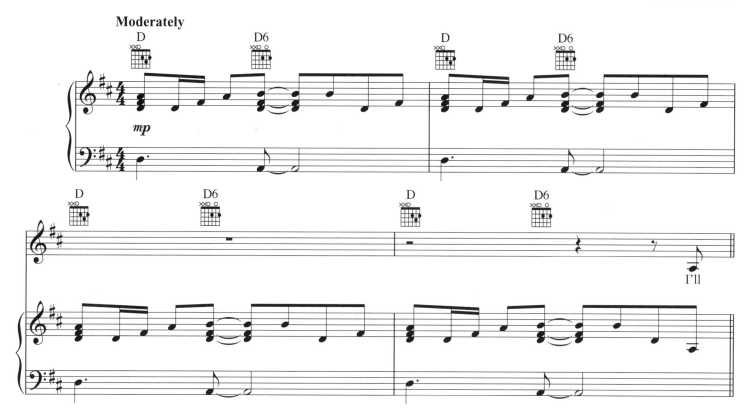

say good-bye ___ to all my sor-row, and by to-mor-row

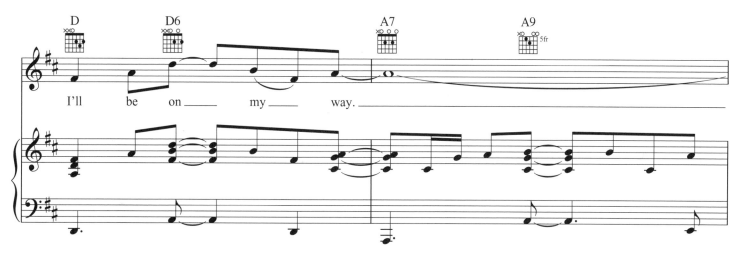

I'll be on ___ my ___ way.

I guess the Lord ___ must be ___ in New York

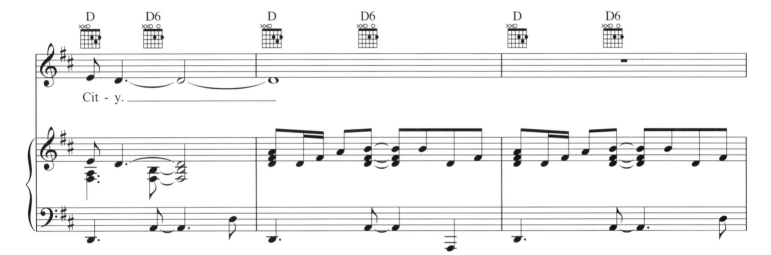

Cit - y. _____

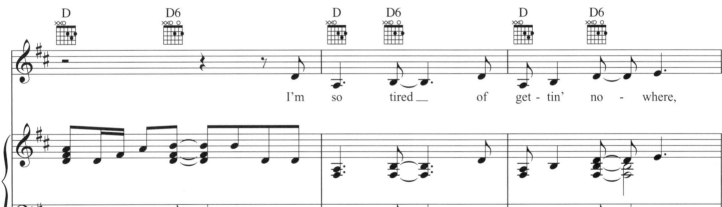

I'm so tired ___ of get - tin' no - where,

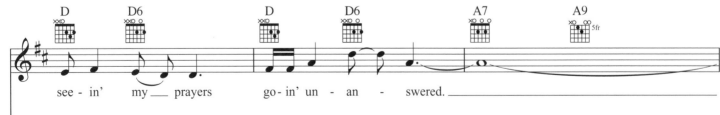

see - in' my ___ prayers go - in' un - an - swered. _____

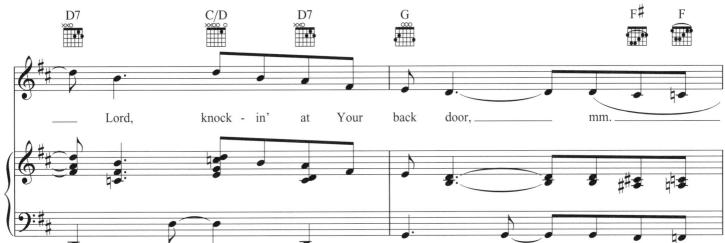

where I've al - ways want - ed to be? ___

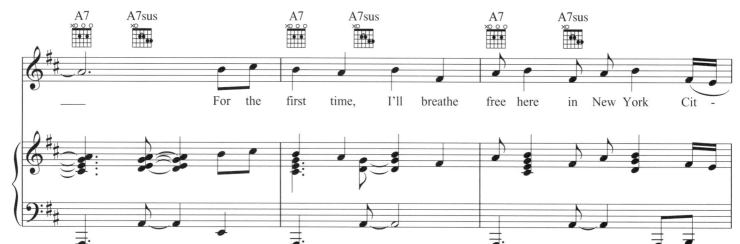

For the first time, I'll breathe free here in New York Cit -

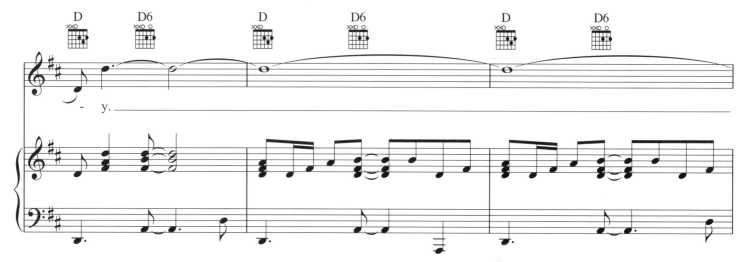

- y. ___

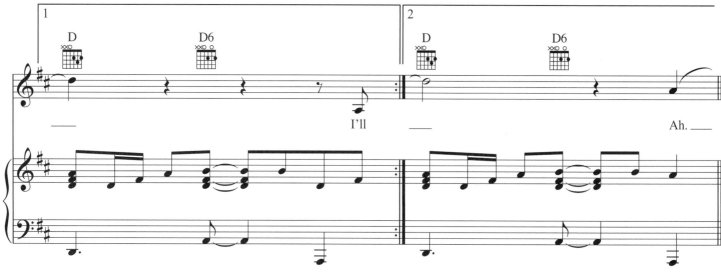

___   I'll ___   Ah. ___

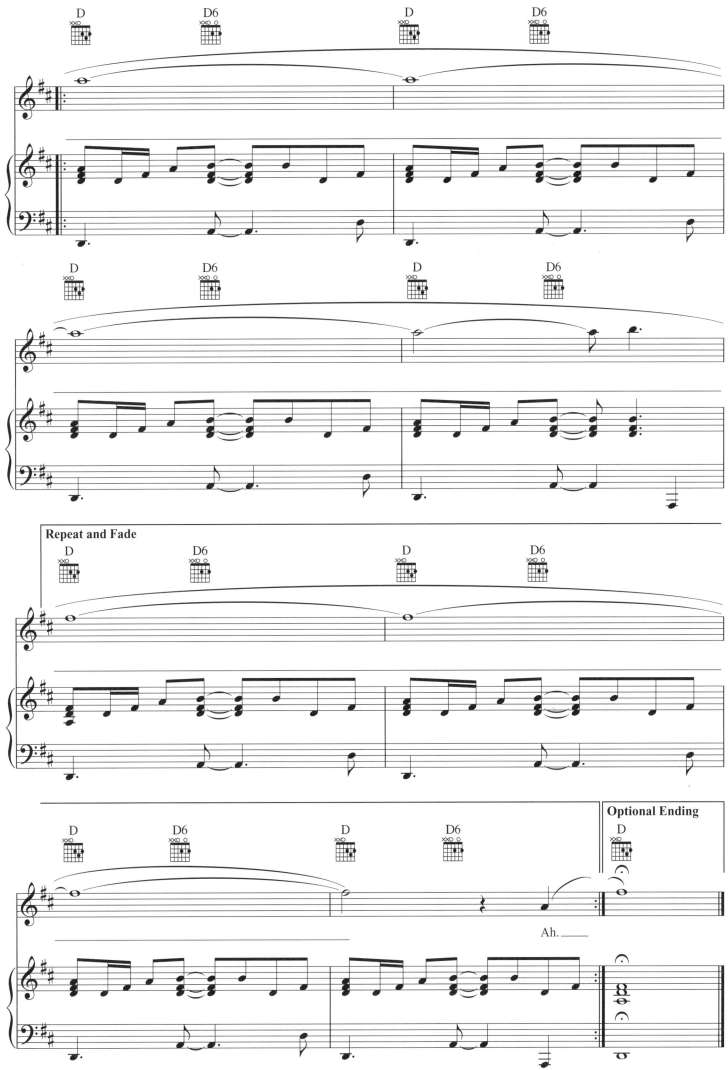

ME AND MY ARROW

Words and Music by
HARRY NILSSON

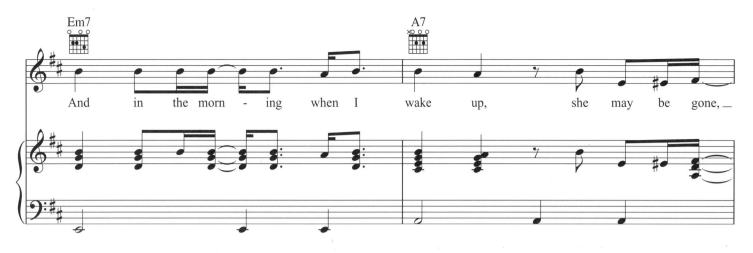

And in the morn-ing when I wake up, she may be gone, ___

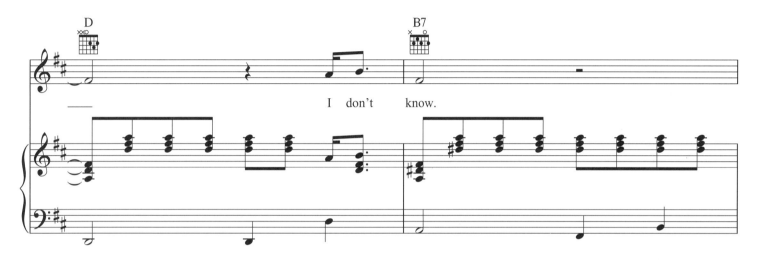

___ I don't know.

And if we make ___ up just to break ___ up, I'll car-ry on, ___

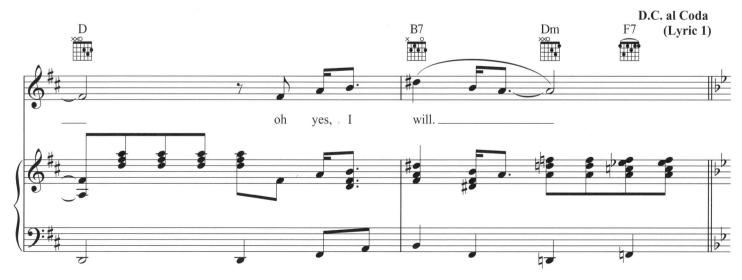

D.C. al Coda
(Lyric 1)

oh yes, I will. ___

CODA

Me and my Ar - row,

me and my Ar - row,

me and my Ar - row, me and my Ar - row,

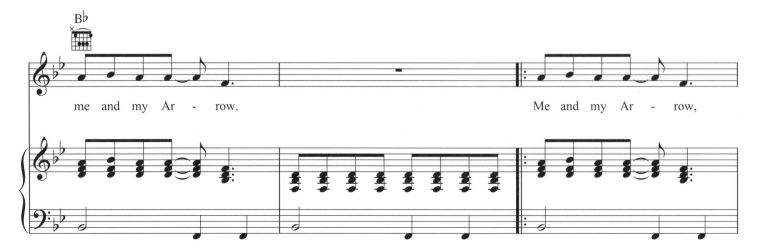

me and my Ar - row.   Me and my Ar - row,

THE MOONBEAM SONG

Words and Music by
HARRY NILSSON

Lazily, in 4

Have you ev - er watched a moon - beam _____ as it slid a - cross your win - dow - pane, _____ or

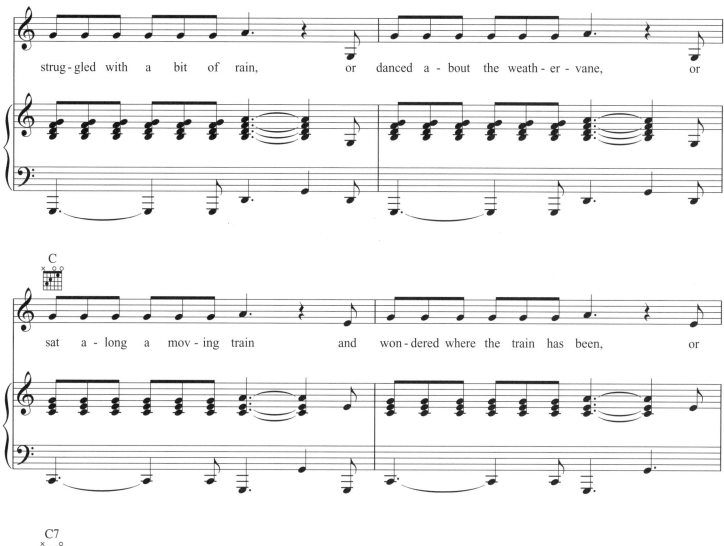

strug-gled with a bit of rain, or danced a-bout the weath-er-vane, or

sat a-long a mov-ing train and won-dered where the train has been, or

on a fence with bits of crap a-round its bot-tom,

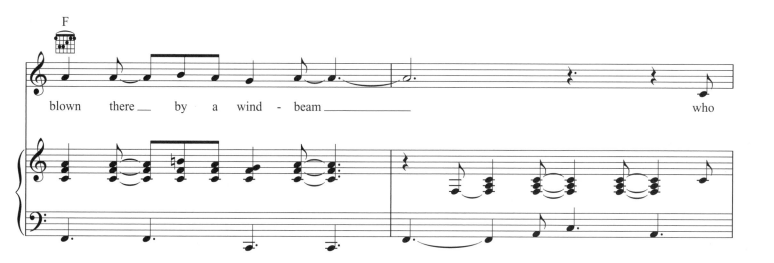

blown there by a wind-beam who

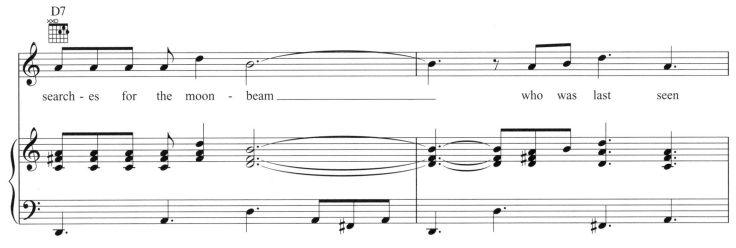

search - es for the moon - beam _____ who was last seen

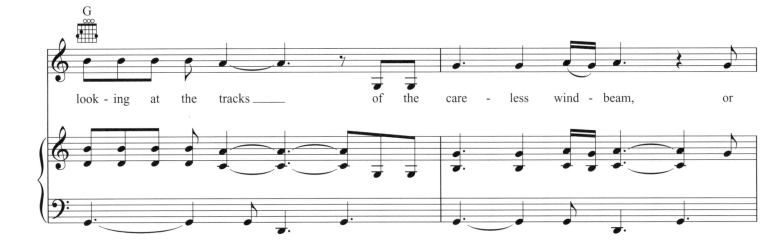

look - ing at the tracks _____ of the care - less wind - beam, or

mov - ing to the tracks of the tire - less freight _ train and

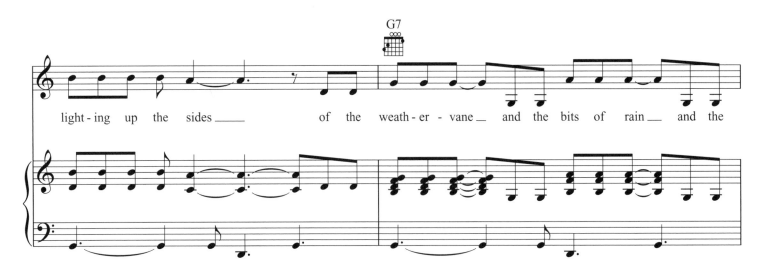

light - ing up the sides _____ of the weath - er - vane _ and the bits of rain _ and the

window-pane ___ and the eyes of those ___ who think they saw what hap - pened? ___

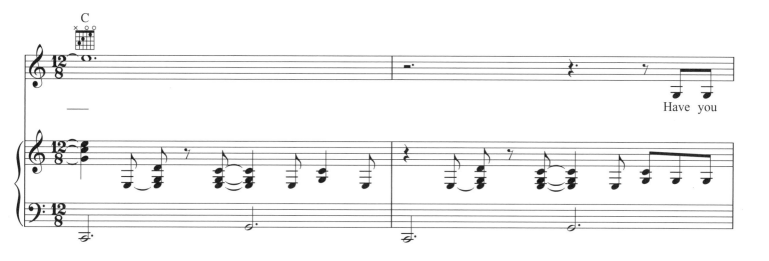

___ Have you

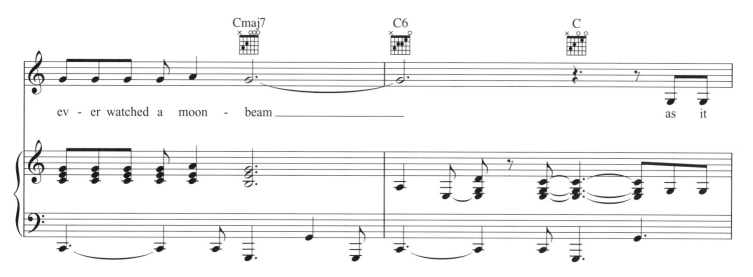

ev - er watched a moon - beam _____ as it

slid a - cross your win - dow - pane, _____ or

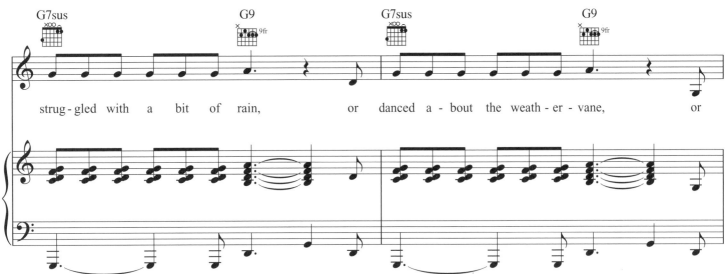

strug-gled with a bit of rain, or danced a-bout the weath-er-vane, or

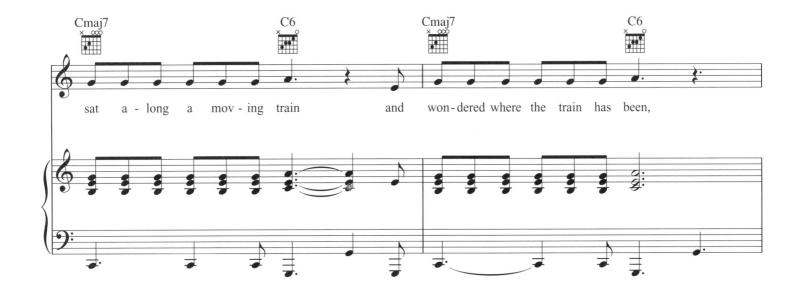

sat a-long a mov-ing train and won-dered where the train has been,

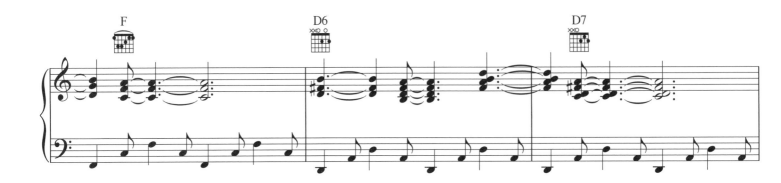

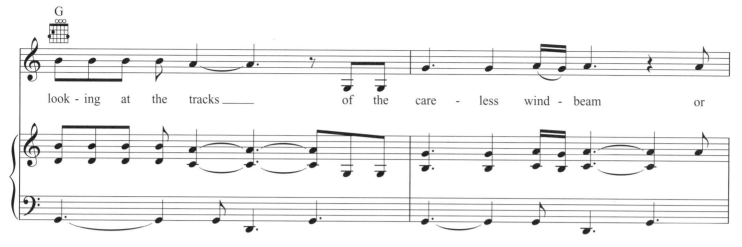

look - ing at the tracks ____ of the care - less wind - beam or

mov - ing to the tracks of the tire - less freight _ train and

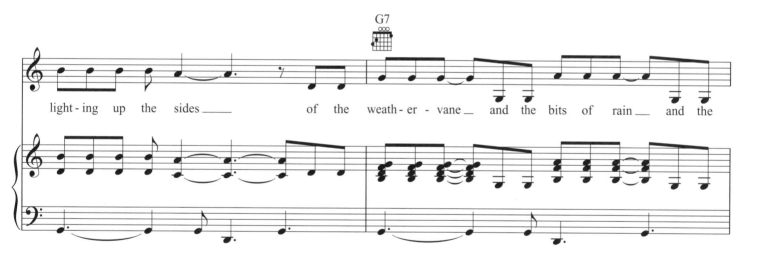

light - ing up the sides ____ of the weath - er - vane ___ and the bits of rain ___ and the

win - dow - pane ___ and the eyes of those ___ who think they saw what hap - pened? ___

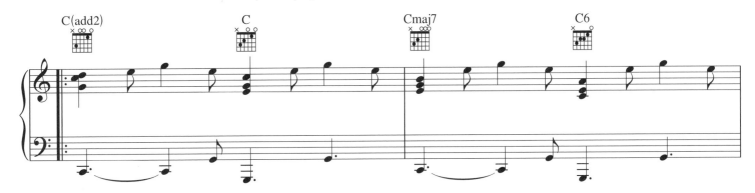

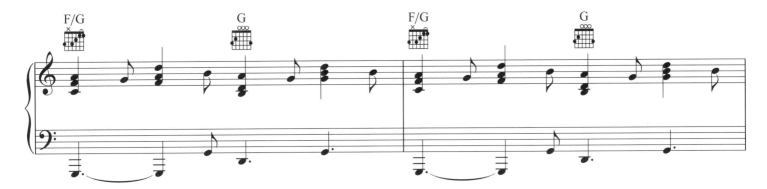

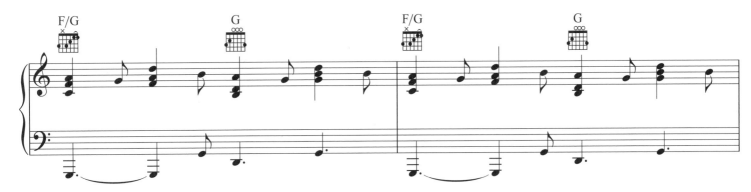

Repeat and Fade | **Optional Ending**

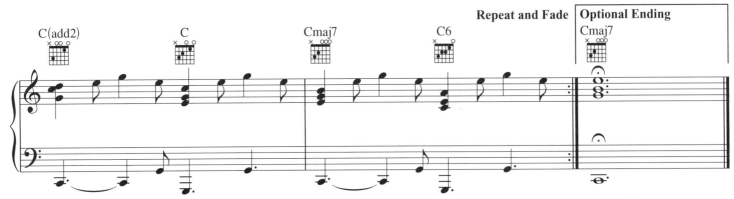

OVER THE RAINBOW
from THE WIZARD OF OZ

Music by HAROLD ARLEN
Lyric by E.Y. "YIP" HARBURG

Slowly

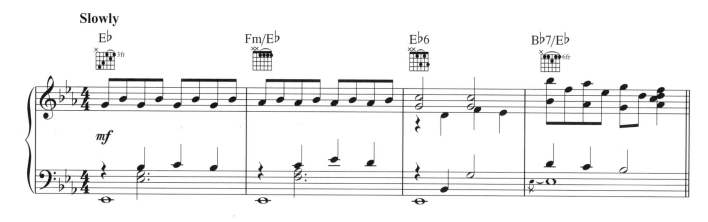

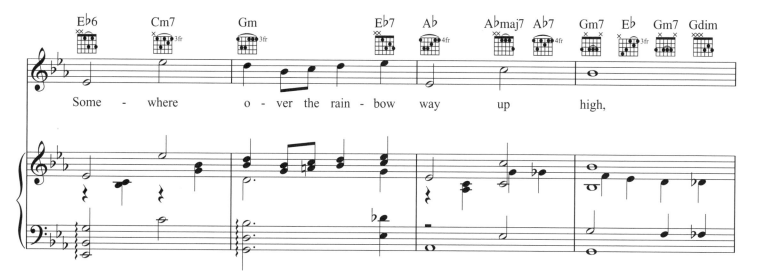

Some - where o - ver the rain - bow way up high,

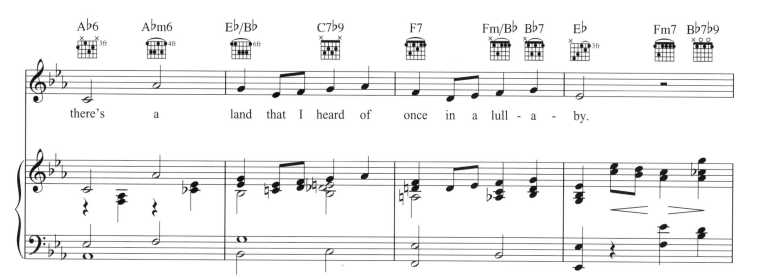

there's a land that I heard of once in a lull - a - by.

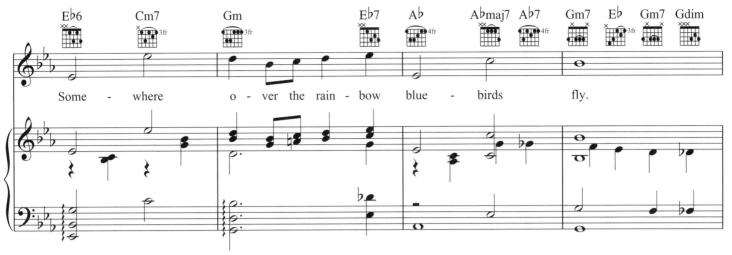

Some - where o - ver the rain - bow blue - birds fly.

Birds fly o - ver the rain - bow, why then, oh why can't I?

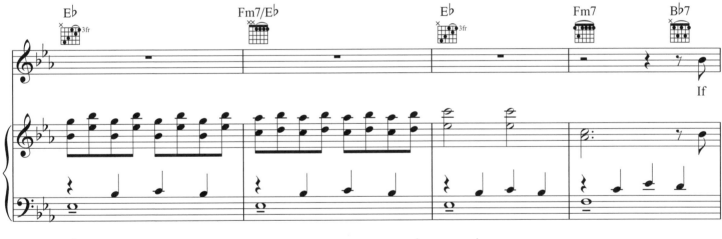

If

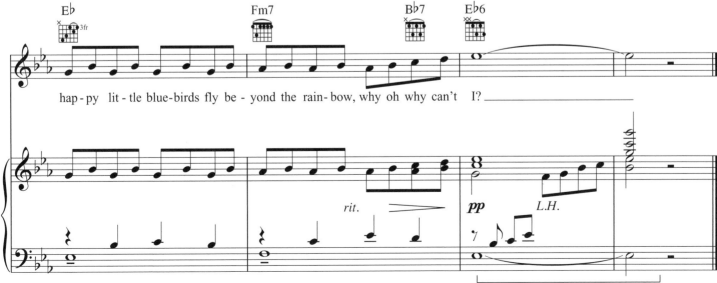

hap - py lit - tle blue-birds fly be - yond the rain-bow, why oh why can't I?

ONE

Words and Music by
HARRY NILSSON

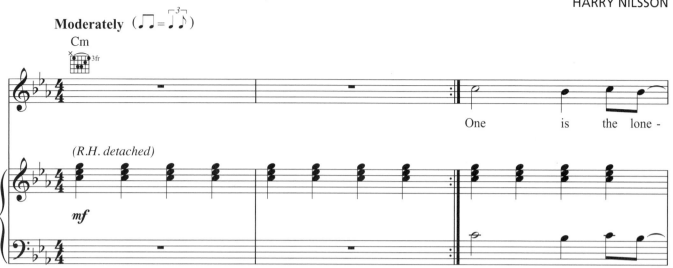

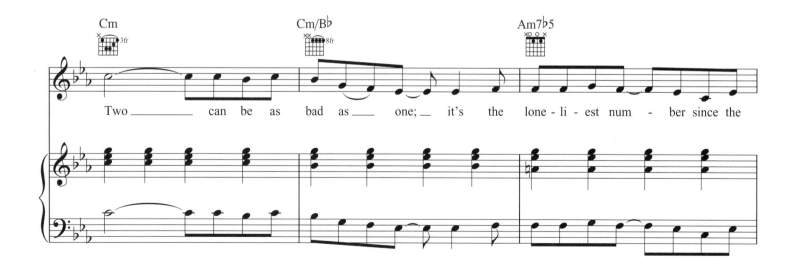

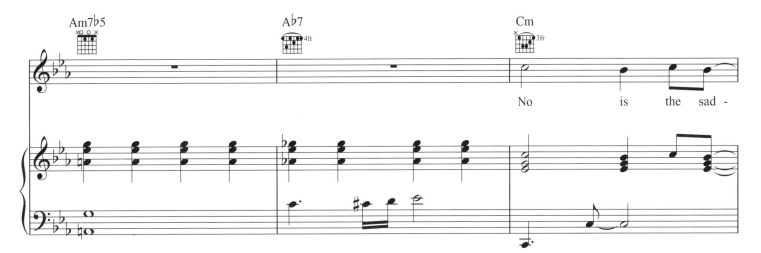

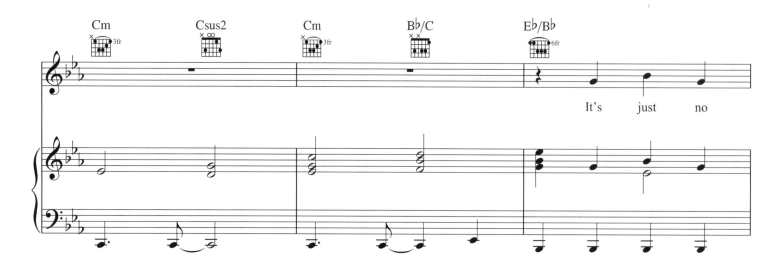

good an-y-more __ since you went a-way. _____ Now I

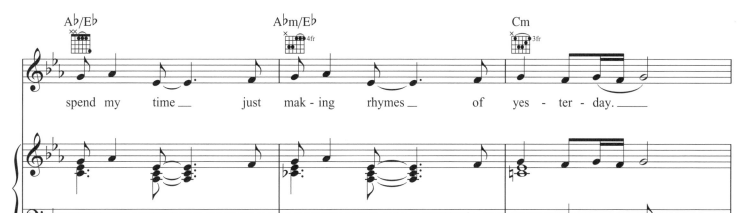

spend my time __ just mak-ing rhymes __ of yes-ter-day. __

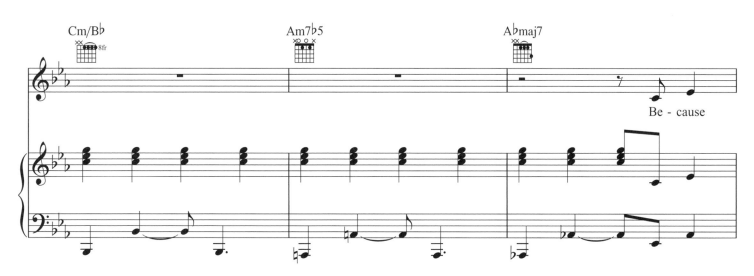

Be-cause

one is the lone-li-est num-ber that you'll ev-er do. __

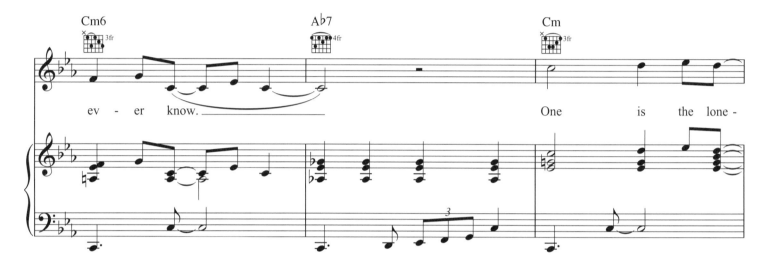

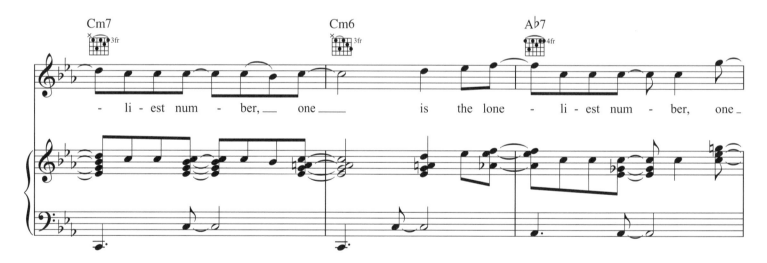

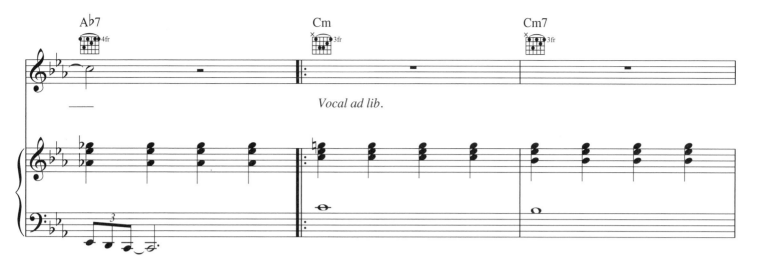

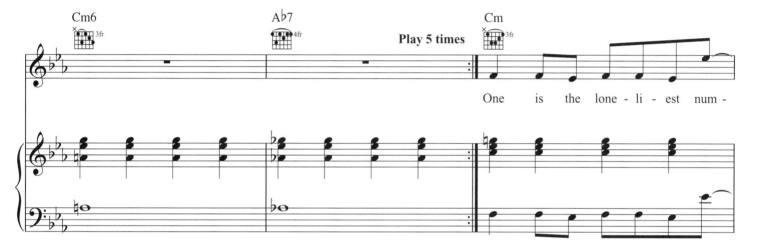

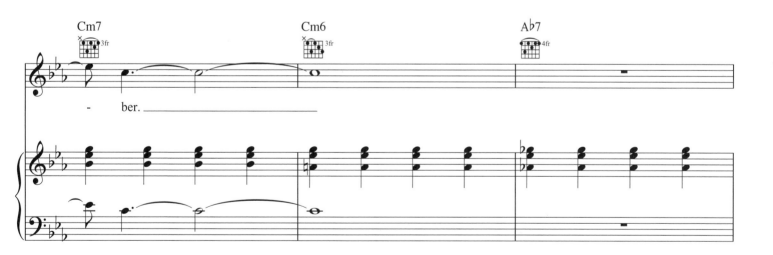

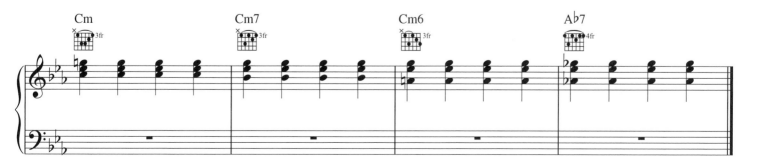

REMEMBER

Words and Music by
HARRY NILSSON

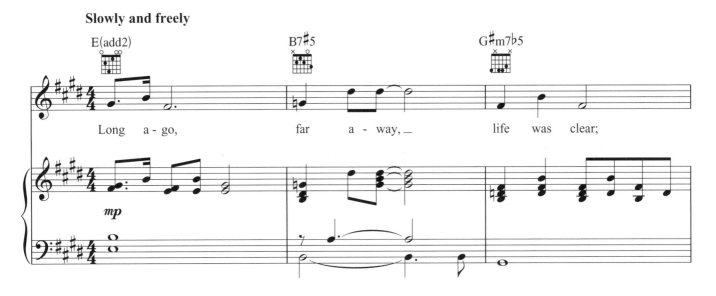

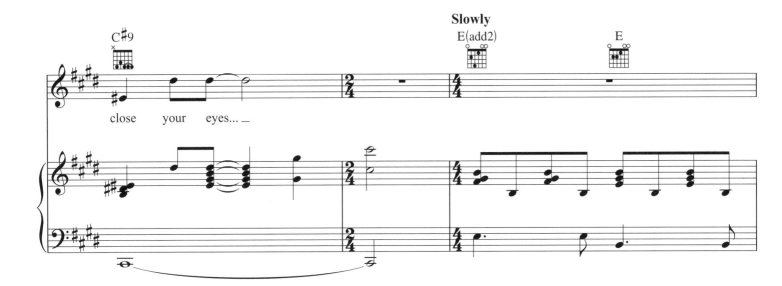

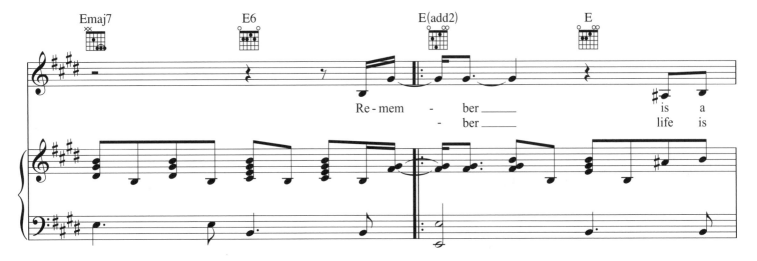

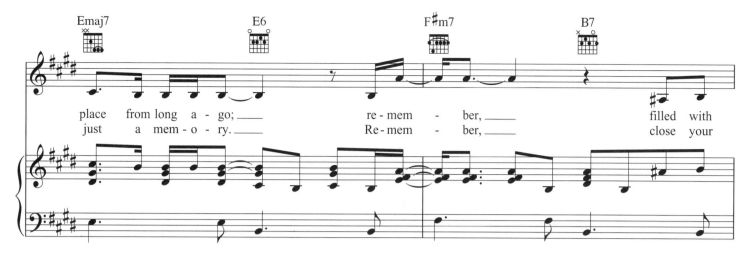

place from long a-go; ____ re-mem - ber, ____ filled with
just a mem-o-ry. ____ Re-mem - ber, ____ close your

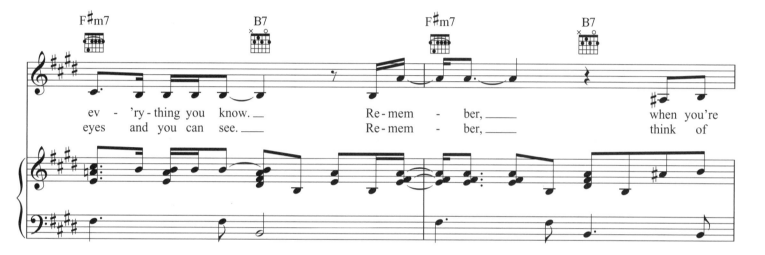

ev-'ry-thing you know. __ Re-mem - ber, ____ when you're
eyes and you can see. __ Re-mem - ber, ____ think of

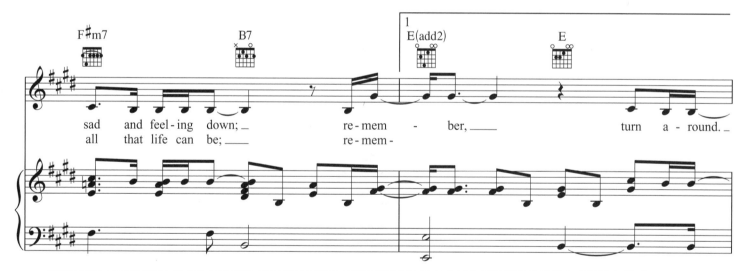

sad and feel-ing down; _ re-mem - ber, ____ turn a-round. _
all that life can be; _ re-mem -

Re-mem - ber. ____

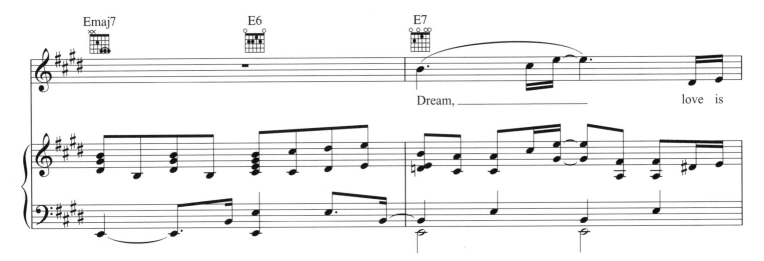

Dream,_____ love is

on - ly in a dream; __ re - mem - ber._____

Re - mem - ber, _____ life is

nev - er as it seems; __ dream..._____

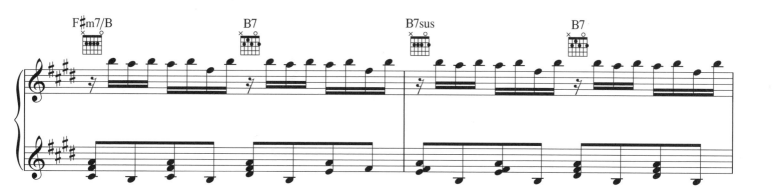

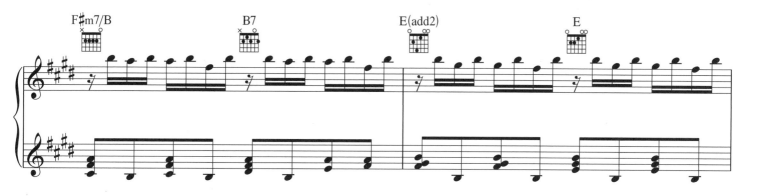

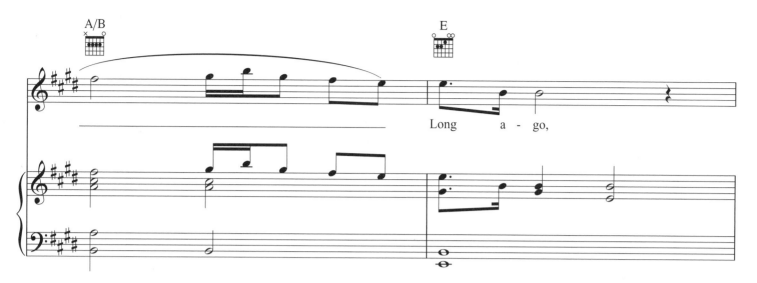

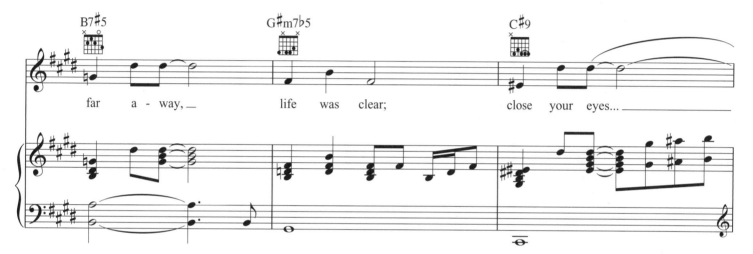

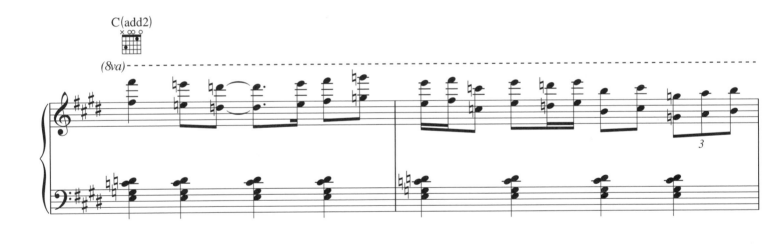

WITHOUT HER

Words and Music by
HARRY NILSSON

do, _____ do, do, do. __ It's just no good an - y - more _ when you walk _

__ thru the door _ of an emp - ty room, _ and then you go in - side _ and set a ta - ble for one. _ It's no

fun when you spend a day with - out ___ her. _____ Do, do, do, _____ do, do, do,

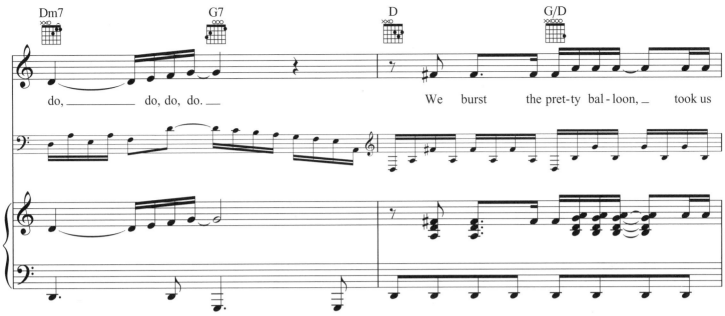

do, _____ do, do, do. ___ We burst the pret-ty bal-loon, _ took us

to the moon; _ such a beau-ti-ful thing. _ But it's end - ed now _ and it sounds _ like a lie __ if I

said I'd rath-er die _____ than _ live with-out her. __ Do, do, do, _____ do, do, do, _

do, _____ do, do, do. ___   *Flute solo*

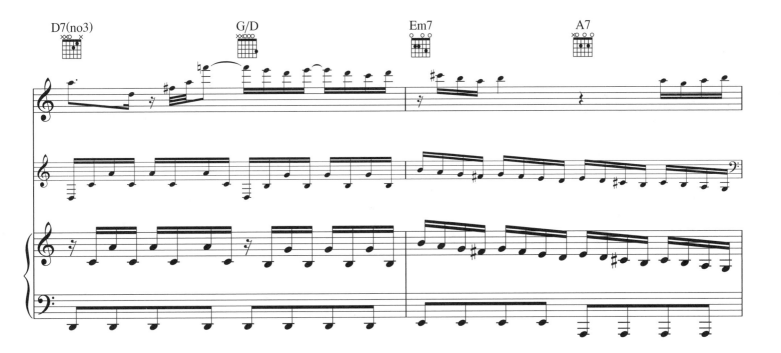

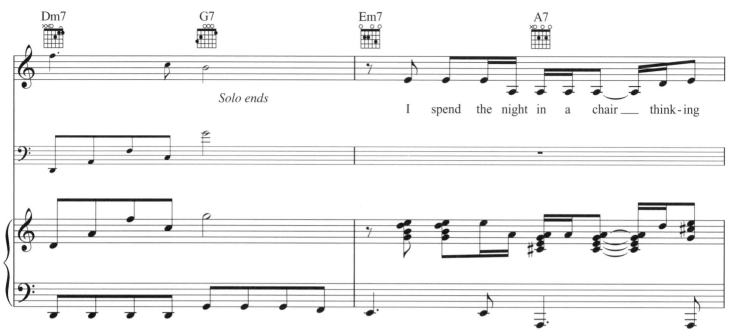

Solo ends

I spend the night in a chair ___ think-ing

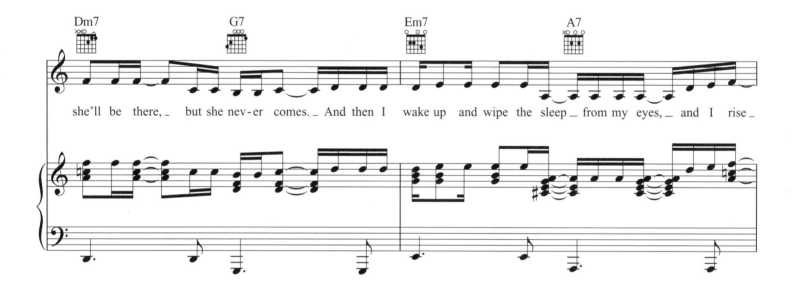

she'll be there, _ but she nev-er comes. _ And then I wake up and wipe the sleep _ from my eyes, _ and I rise _

___ to face an-oth-er day ___ with - out her. ___ Do, do, do, ___ do, do, do,
(Vocal ad lib. on repeat)

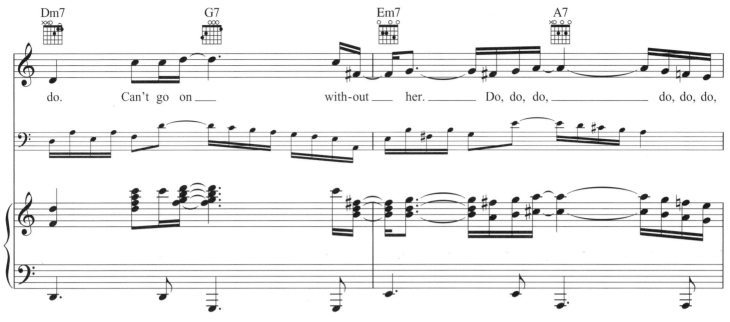

do. Can't go on ___ with-out ___ her. ___ Do, do, do, ___ do, do, do,

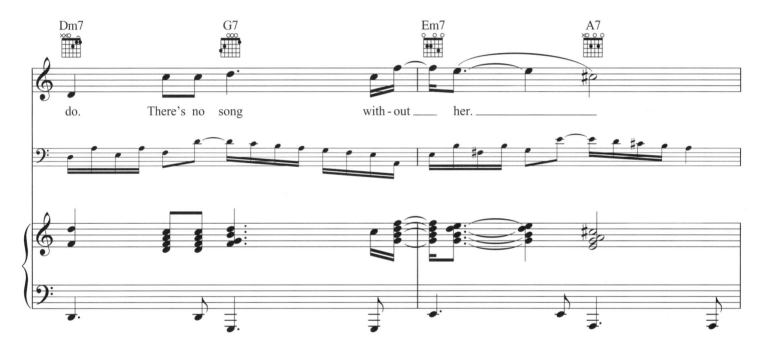

do. There's no song with - out ___ her. ___

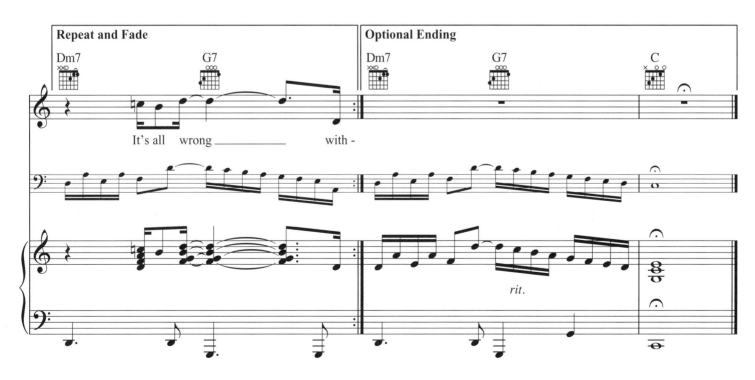

Repeat and Fade

It's all wrong _____ with -

Optional Ending

rit.

WITHOUT YOU

Words and Music by PETER HAM
and THOMAS EVANS

Moderately slow

No, I can't for-get __ this eve-ning or your

face as you were leav-ing, but I guess that's just the way the sto-ry

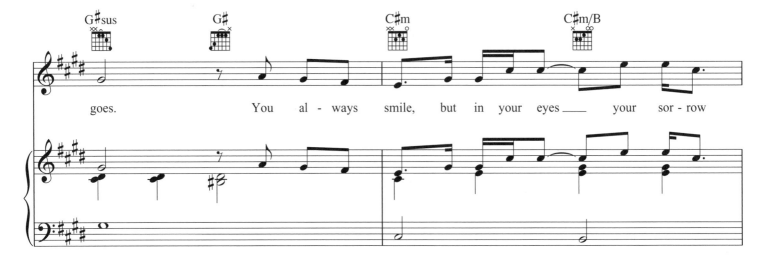

goes. You al-ways smile, but in your eyes __ your sor-row

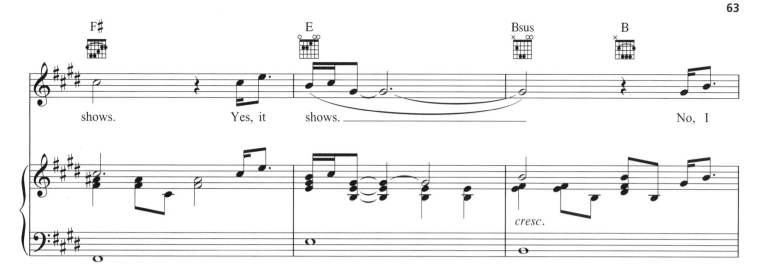

shows.   Yes, it   shows. _____   No, I

can't for-get ___ to-mor-row when I   think of all ___ my sor-row, when I
can't for-get ___ this eve-ning or your   face as you ___ were leav-ing, but I

had you there, _ but then I let you go.   And now it's
guess that's just ___ the way the sto - ry goes.   You al - ways

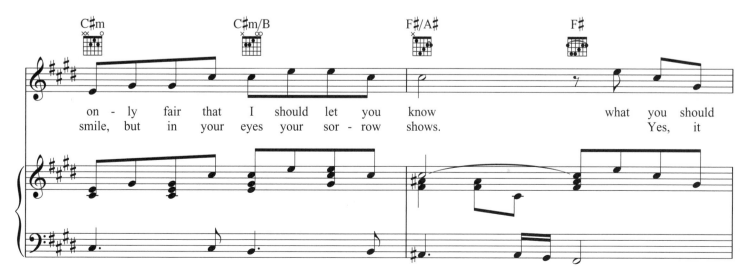

on - ly fair that I should let you know   what you should
smile, but in your eyes your sor - row shows.   Yes, it

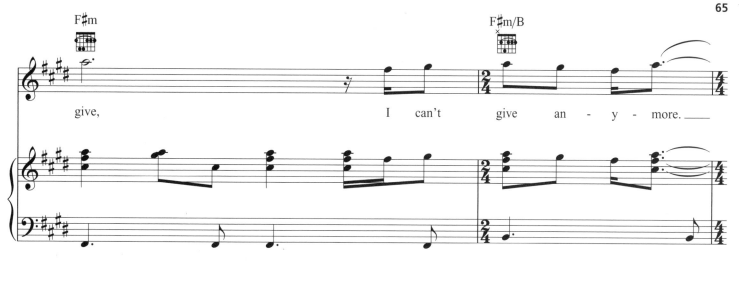

give, I can't give an - y - more.____

D.S. al Coda

____ Well, I

CODA B7

____ I can't

cresc.

E   C#m

live _____ if liv - ing is with - out you._____ I can't

f

Repeat ad lib. and Fade **Optional Ending**

F#m   F#m/B   E

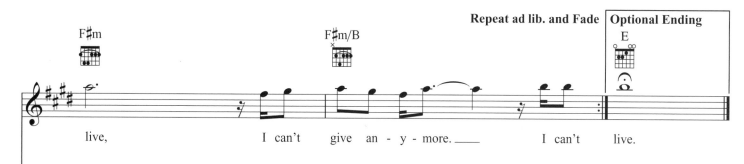

live, I can't give an - y - more.____ I can't live.

YOU'RE BREAKIN' MY HEART

Words and Music by
HARRY NILSSON

Honky-Tonk Rock

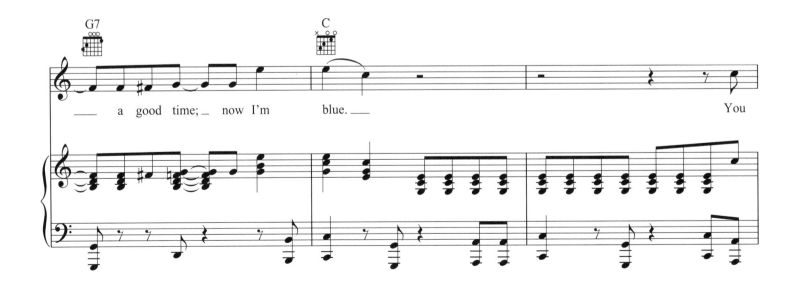

wan-na boo - ga - loo, ___ run down to Tramps, ___ have a dance or two, ___

___ ooh. ___ You're break - in' my heart, ___ you're tear-in' it a - part, ___ but f***

you. You're break - in' my heart, ___ you're

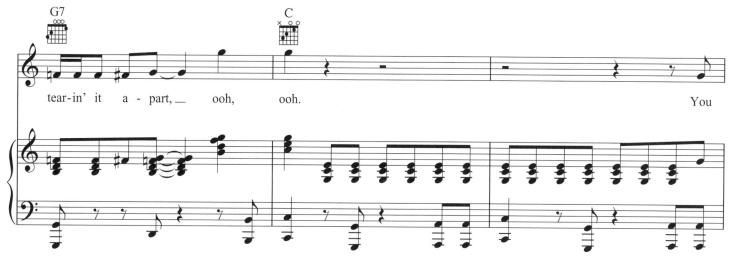

tear-in' it a - part, ___ ooh, ooh. You

stepped on my ass, _____ you're break-in' my glass - es, too. _____

You wan-na drive my car, ___ buy a lot of stuff. _

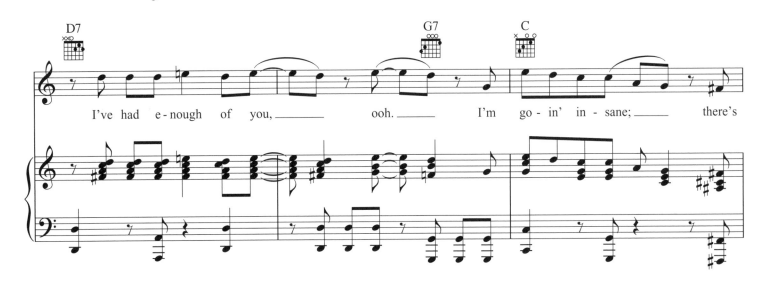

I've had e-nough of you, _____ ooh. _____ I'm go-in' in-sane; _____ there's

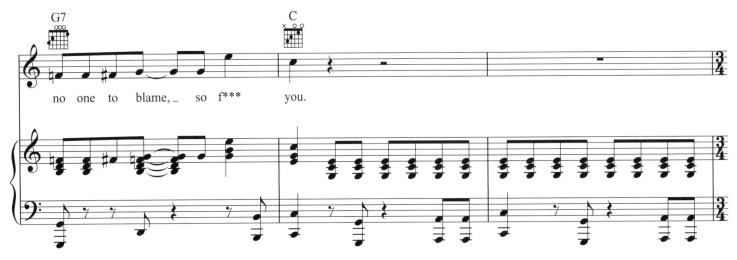

no one to blame, _ so f*** you.

ooh. _____ You're break-in' my heart, _ you're tear-in' it a-part, _ so f***

you.

You've got-ta have your way; _ there's noth-in' left to say, _

there's noth-ing left to do, _____ ooh. _____ You're break-in' my heart, _ you're

tear-in' it a-part, _ but I _____ love _____ you.

Do, do, do, do, do, do, do, do, do, _____ do, _____ do, _____ do. _____

Repeat and Fade   **Optional Ending**

SPACEMAN

Words and Music by
HARRY NILSSON

want-ed to be ___ a space-man. That's what I want - ed to be. But

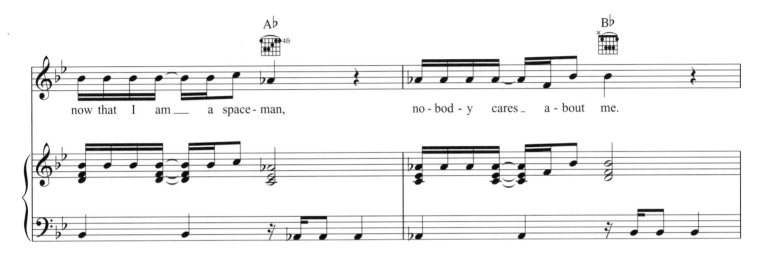

now that I am ___ a space-man, no - bod - y cares ___ a - bout me.

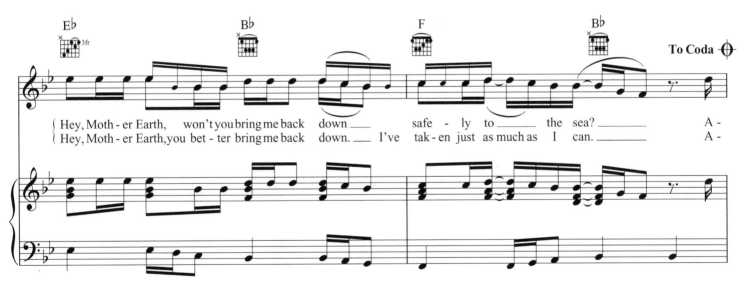

Hey, Moth - er Earth, won't you bring me back down ___ safe - ly to ___ the sea? ___ A -

Hey, Moth - er Earth, you bet - ter bring me back down. ___ I've tak - en just as much as I can. ___ A -

To Coda ⊕

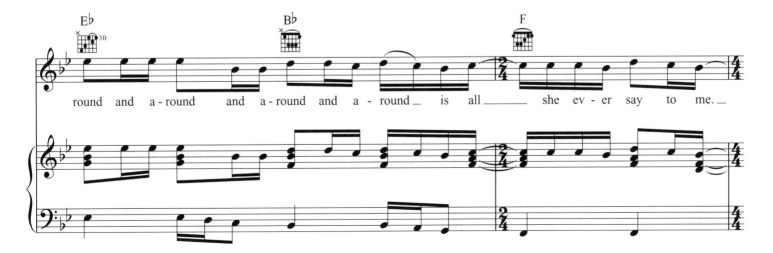

round and a - round and a - round and a - round ___ is all ___ she ev - er say to me. ___

want-ed to make a good run. I want-ed to go to the moon. I

knew that it had to be fun. I told 'em to send me real soon. I

want-ed to be a space-man. I want-ed to be it so bad. But

now that I am ___ a space-man, _____ I'd rath-er be back ___ on the pad.

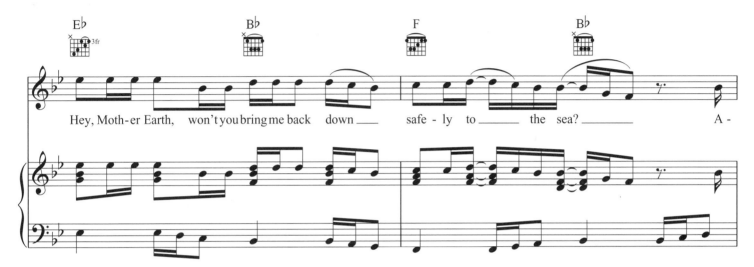

Hey, Moth-er Earth, won't you bring me back down ___ safe-ly to _____ the sea? _____ A-

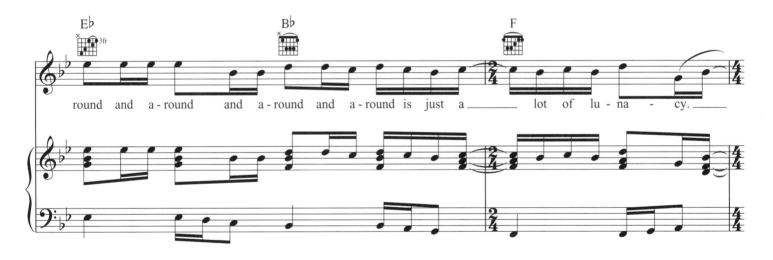

round and a-round and a-round and a-round is just a _____ lot of lu-na-cy. _____

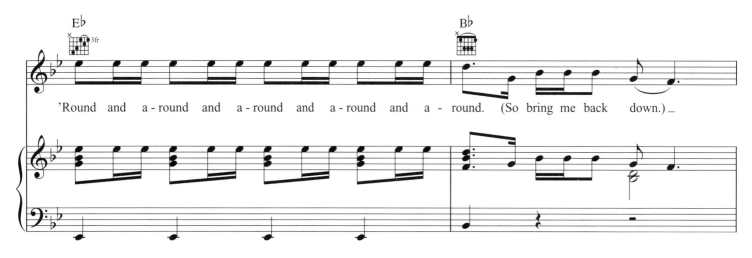

'Round and a-round and a-round and a-round and a-round. (So bring me back down.) __

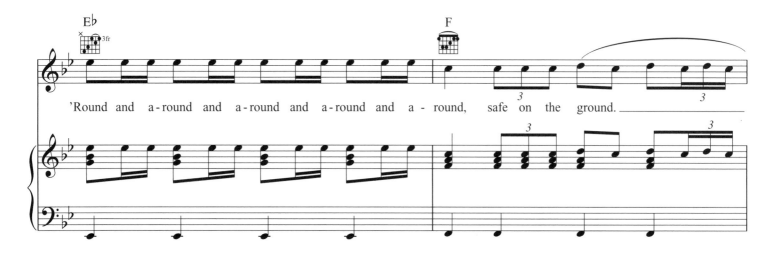

'Round and a-round and a-round and a-round and a-round, safe on the ground. __

__ Ooh, ooh, __ ooh, ooh, __ ooh, ooh, __ ooh.

Ooh, ooh, ooh, __ ooh, ooh, __ ooh, __ ooh, __ ooh.

Ooh, ooh, ooh, _____ ooh, ooh, _____ ooh, _____ ooh, _____ ooh.

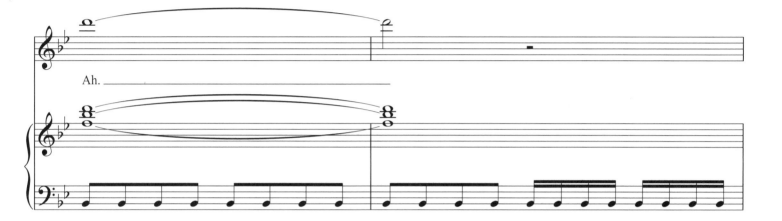

Ah. _____

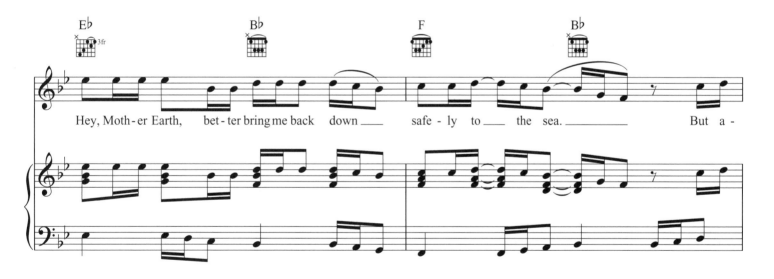

Hey, Moth-er Earth, bet-ter bring me back down _____ safe-ly to _____ the sea. _____ But a-

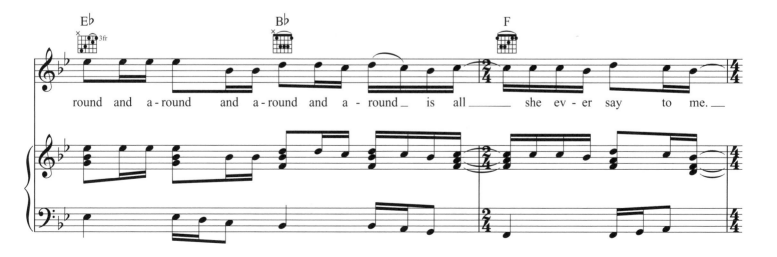

round and a-round and a-round and a-round _____ is all _____ she ev-er say to me. ___

D.S. al Coda

You know, I

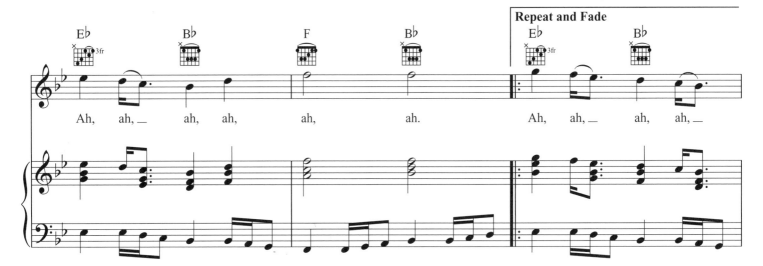

CODA

round and a-round and a-round and a-round __ is the prob-lem for the space-man. __

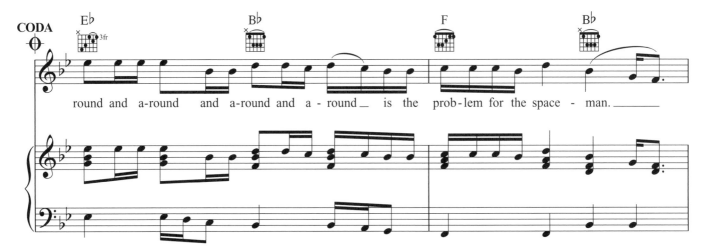

Repeat and Fade

Ah, ah, __ ah, ah, ah, ah. Ah, ah, __ ah, ah, __

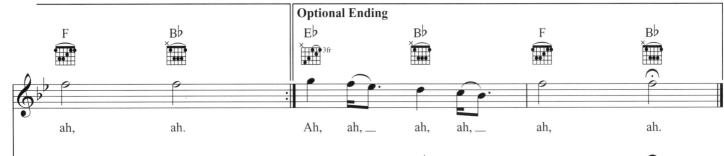

Optional Ending

ah, ah. Ah, ah, __ ah, ah, __ ah, ah.